Hurghada Travel Guide

Sightseeing, Hotel, Restaurant & Shopping Highlights

Rebecca Kaye

Copyright © 2014, Astute Press
All Rights Reserved.

No part of this publication may be reproduced, stored in a retrieval system, or transmitted, in any form or by any means without the prior written permission of the publisher, nor be otherwise circulated in any form of binding or cover other than that in which it is published and without similar condition being imposed on the subsequent purchaser.

If there are any errors or omissions in copyright acknowledgements the publisher will be pleased to insert the appropriate acknowledgement in any subsequent printing of this publication.

Although we have taken all reasonable care in researching this book we make no warranty about the accuracy or completeness of its content and disclaim all liability arising from its use

Table of Contents

Hurghada 6
    Culture 7
    Location & Orientation 9
    Climate & When to Visit 10
Sightseeing Highlights 11
    New Marina 11
    El Dahar 12
    Water Parks 13
        Makadi Waterworld 13
        Sindbad Aqua Park 14
        Jungle Aqua Park 15
    Churches & Mosques 15
    Encounters with Dolphins 16
    Red Sea Scuba Diving 17
        Diving Preparation 18
        Reef Diving 18
        Shipwreck Diving 19
        Giftun Islands 21
        Diving Locations Nearby 21
    Resorts near Hurghada 22
        Makadi Bay 22
        El Gouna 23
        Sahl Hasheesh 24
        Soma Bay 25
        Port Safaga 25
    Nightlife in Hurghada 26
    Day Trips 27
Recommendations for the Budget Traveller 28
    Places to Stay 28
        Triton Empire Inn 28
        Movenpick Resort Hurghada 29
        Sol y Mar Ivory Suites 30
        Magawish Swiss Inn Resort 30
        Festival Riviera 31
    Places to Eat 32

    Nubian Cafe & Restaurant 32
    El Mina Restaurant 33
    The Lodge Restaurant 33
    Moby Dick 34
    La Trattoria 34
Places to Shop 35
    Downtown Bazaar 35
    Hurghada Star Shop 35
    Shopping at the New Marina 36
    Senzo Mall 37
    Cleopatra Center 38

Hurghada

Hurghada is Egypt's seaside paradise for water lovers of all ages. Dive into the Red Sea and experience the colourful wonderland of coral and vividly patterned marine species. At Hurghada, nature's richest bounty is seen below the water's surface and many visitors come to dive or snorkel.

Hurghada is located along a coastal strip of land sometimes referred to as the Egyptian Riviera. It combines the marine and seaside amusements of a resort beside the Red sea, with easy access to some of Egypt's most famous ancient attractions.

The city can be used as a base for day trips to Luxor, Ancient Thebes, the Nile and even Cairo. You could also explore the formidable desert via camel safari, quad bike excursions or through a regular bus tour and interact with the enigmatic Bedouin tribespeople.

Most hotels and resorts in the area offer access to scuba diving and snorkelling activities. Several of the larger hotels also have stables and include horse-riding in their range of available amusements. Other popular activities are golf, camel riding and windsurfing. Several hotel groups have their own waterparks and at night, you can party at one of several popular night spots. Hurghada has several modern shopping centers, but also supports more traditional trading, at markets, bazaars, souqs and street vendors.

By Egyptian standards, Hurghada is still in its infancy. It was only founded in the 20th century, but thanks to favorable conditions, the city has grown rapidly from a humble fishing village to a popular holiday resort with a population of around 248,000. It has become a favorite holiday spot for both domestic and international tourists, particularly Italians, Russians and Germans.

Culture

Egyptian people are predominantly described as Eastern Hamite, which includes Egyptian, Berber and Bedouin blood in their heritage. There is a very small percentage of Europeans, mainly of Italian and French extraction. The official language is Arabic, but English and French is also generally understood.

Egyptians are peace-loving and the concept of family plays a large role in everyday life. The patriarch of the family usually has the final authority in decisions. As the eldest male representative, this could be the father or eldest surviving son. Respect for the person who represents this position, is entrenched in everyday culture. Female tourists, especially those travelling alone, are advised to be cautious in their interactions with male Egyptians, as harassment can be a real problem in certain situations. In general, though, tourists are treated very well by people within the hospitality industry, as the country's economy relies heavily on revenue from tourism. The southern Red Sea region has remained peaceful despite political unrest in other parts of the country.

Egypt's population is predominantly Sunni Muslim. A smaller portion of the population is Christian. Most Egyptian Christians are members of the Coptic Church, a church that dates back to the 1st century AD and is associated with St Mark, founder of the Church of Alexandria. The population are generally tolerant of foreigners. While the dress code in resort areas are generally more relaxed, topless bathing and public drunkenness is frowned upon.

Visitors who enjoy a beer or two, will be heartened to know that there are a number of venues that serve alcohol. Egypt even has a few beer brands of its own and several types of wine. Brewed since 1897, Stella is the best known and most popular brand of beer. Cru des Ptolmees is an aromatic wine allegedly based on a wine recipe Cleopatra enjoyed.

Another typically Egyptian wine is Abarka, which is used by the Christian Copts at Christmas and around Easter. At 16 percent, it has a slightly higher alcohol content than most wines. Whiskey lovers may wish to sample Auld Stag, a blended whiskey that Egypt exports to several other countries.

The most popular entertainer in Egypt is Mohamed Mounir, an actor and singer who is sometimes referred to as "The King of Egypt". Another significant musician of Egypt is the folk singer Ahmed Mounib.

Location & Orientation

Hurghada is located along the western shore of the Red Sea. It stretches along the coast some 36km, but does not extend far into the desert interior. It lies south of the Suez Canal and about 550km from Cairo.

The city can be divided into three sections. The oldest part is El Dahar or Downtown, where you can expect to encounter the city's largest bazaar, as well as the post office and the terminal for long distance bus travel. Sekella is an important hotel sector, whereas the area referred to as El Korra Road includes some of the city's most modern developments.

With regards to air travel, Hurghada has an international airport, which offers connecting flights from Cairo, as well as direct flights from several cities on the European continent. In fact, Hurghada is just a four hour flight away from several major European centers.

If you are planning to rent a car, be advised that the traffic in Egypt can get extremely chaotic. Egypt's most popular dive location, Sharm El-Sheikh, is also accessible from Hurghada, via a 90 minute ferry cruise.

Climate & When to Visit

Hurghada has a sub-tropical desert climate. It enjoys warm, sunny weather year round, with day temperatures in summer rising to above 35 degrees Celsius in summer and remaining around 30 degrees Celsius even at night. From June to September, the weather is sweltering and even during October, day temperatures may still average above 30 degrees Celsius.

In the winter months, between December and February, the weather is cooler, with temperatures typically fluctuating between 24 and 22 degrees Celsius and sometimes dropping as low as 19 or even 16 degrees Celsius at night-time. The region sees very little rainfall, with November being the wettest month at a minimal 3.8mm.

In springtime, during late March and April, huge flocks of migratory birds can be seen passing through the skies above Egypt. March, however, is also the windiest month in Hurghada. Anyone wishing to enjoy one of the city's many water-based activities, will want to come when the water is at its warmest, between May and October. Generally, Hurghada is most crowded during July and August, as those months coincide with school holidays in Europe.

Sightseeing Highlights

New Marina

http://www.hurghadamarinaredsea.com/

The New Marina development gave Hurghada a facelift, combining wide, palm-lined walkways with a range of upmarket shops, bars and restaurants. Visitors can enjoy the tranquil, view of the mosque or feast their eyes on rows of luxury yachts in the millionaire's row. The marina can offer berthing to up to 200 yachts.

Adrenaline junkies will be drawn to the thrill of the 42m high Rocket Bungee, while those seeking refreshments can choose from restaurants, bars and cafes that serve a wide variety of cuisine styles from around the world. The marina is also a great place to organize boat tours or diving excursions. Challenge provides a bouncing castle for kids, but also offers visitors the opportunity of enjoying a fun wrestling bout with inflatable props and soft battle sticks. It is located opposite Papa's Bar.

The marina development also has a 7D cinema theatre that offers viewers the sensation of feeling fog, snow, rain and wind in an exciting virtual reality simulation. Other attractions include an art gallery and a fish spa. By night, visitors can party at Papa's Beach Club or relax at Friends Bar or the Lodge Bar. The original Papas Bar is a lively venue that offers a variety of entertainment options, including live music, big screen broadcasts during major sport events and quiz contests.

El Dahar

If you wish to experience a slice of Egyptian life, visit El Dahar, the older, downtown section of Hurghada. The post office and the tourist office are located here. There are plenty of shops, markets, restaurants and clubs and the area comes to life after dark. Don't be shy to haggle with the traders, if you are looking for a bargain, but do bear in mind that Egyptian vendors can be rather aggressive in their sales pitch.

Also in El Dahar, is the Aquarium, which is located near the main hospital. While this was once regarded as a great place to identify different species you are likely to encounter on a diving drip, the general sentiment now is that nothing beats seeing marine species in their natural habitat.

Water Parks

There are several water parks in and around Hurghada, each of them built in association with a particular hotel group. Special rates are offered to guests, but the facilities are open to the public at a slightly higher rate.

Makadi Waterworld

Makadi Bay, Madinat Makadi, Hurghada, Egypt
http://www.jaz.travel/madinat-makadi-water.aspx

As one of the largest waterparks in Africa, Makadi Water World offers a safe, fun-filled environment with attractions to suit the whole family. The setting is bright and colorfully decorated. One popular themed section is known as the pirate area. Here, you can expect to find vividly rendered pirate sculptures and ships and, if you fancy a cool-off, a dip under the pirate's bucket is recommended.

Overall, the park has more than 50 rides, which include multiple lane slides, the family ring slide and several creatively looped and intertwined tunnel slides, which feature interesting and challenging twists and curves. One highlight is a 19m freefall slide. For those who just want to relax, there are several pools and plenty of sun loungers, as well as a beautifully laid out garden with plenty of tall palm trees. There is also a food section which offers burgers, pizza, waffles, sandwiches and ice cream and a special area for toddlers. Do bring sunblock and waterproof shoes, as the sun can be rather fierce and the marble floors slippery when wet.

Sindbad Aqua Park

Sindbad Club, Hurghada, Egypt
Tel: +2 065 944 9601-7
http://www.sindbadclub.com/aqua-park

Sindbad Aqua Park is an up-to-date facility set in inviting tropical surrounds. Although smaller than the other two water parks, Sindbad Aqua Park does offer a number of thrilling slides. The big attraction is the Boomerango, which includes a steep slope and can be enjoyed in a single or double tube. Adventurous visitors will also enjoy the Sky Dive and the High Thrill, both of which offer a speedy course full of excitement. For kids, there is the Toods Pool and Play Pond. Relax in the Blue Lagoon, an enormous wave pool that includes an artificial beach and tropical palm trees. The attraction is administered by the Sindbad Club, a group that includes the Sindbad Beach Resort, Sindbad Aqua Hotel and the Sindbad Aqua Resort.

Jungle Aqua Park

Jungle Aqua Park Hotel, Safaga Road, Hurghada
Tel: +20 65 3464670

The Jungle Aqua Park is a facility of the hotel of the same name. The landscaped garden features sculptures of various wild animals, including the zebra and the hippo and the area has plenty of sun loungers for relaxing. There are 21 pools and 6 different restaurants, as well as 35 slides, of which 14 are tailored for kids, while the other 21 offer thrills for teens and adults.

Churches & Mosques

There are a few places of worship in Hurghada, each with a structural elegance that blends beautifully with the surrounding landscape. The Coptic church, also known as the Cathedral of Saint Shemoun, is characterized by elegant lines, and gently curving detail. This building can be viewed inside, providing this does not interfere with religious ceremonies. No admission is charged, but donations are welcome. El Mina Mosque is of recent construction and can be visited by tourists outside the designated prayer times. It is easily accessible, thanks to its location right beside the marina. The interior features beautifully detailed artwork. Do remember to dress respectfully.

Encounters with Dolphins

Several species of dolphin inhabit the Red Sea. These include two varieties of bottlenose dolphin, the Spinner dolphin and Risso's dolphin. Spinner dolphins often congregate around offshore reefs, while bottlenose dolphins prefer coastal waters. Their intelligence and friendliness make them a popular draw card for visitors to the Red Sea in general and Hurghada in particular.

There are generally two types of dolphin encounters. The one typically involves a one-hour show which displays the skills of trained dolphins, usually with an opportunity to briefly interact with the dolphins. The other type of dolphin encounter is more spontaneous and occurs when you are taken to a location known to be frequented by wild dolphins, for a diving or snorkelling experience. Animal welfare groups have expressed their concern and opposition to the former type of dolphin attraction.

At Dolphinella, you can enjoy a guided tour, which is available in various languages including English, Russian, German and Italian. The experience includes 30 minutes of close interaction with the facility's three resident dolphins. At $190, the tours are quite expensive, but this is partly because numbers are limited to two persons per tour. Book early to avoid disappointment. A soft drink and hotel transfers are included in the price. Bring sunblock and comfortable walking shoes.

An encounter at sea will be less predictable, but ultimately more rewarding. You could book a special dolphin-spotting cruise (http://www.oceansredsea.com/hurghada.html), but sometimes, it is possible to get lucky on a regular excursion to one of the reefs in the area.

Red Sea Scuba Diving

The Red Sea was formed millions of years ago, when the Arabian Peninsula split off from Africa, forming the Red Sea Rift. Why is it called the Red Sea? According to historians, that may have simply been relative to its location in the south. In ancient times, the cardinal directions were often associated with different colors. The Red Sea facilitated part of Roman naval trade, and later became an important section of the medieval spice trade.

Due to surface water temperatures between 26 and 30 degrees in summer, sparse rainfall and practically no fresh water sources, the Red Sea is one of the saltiest bodies of water on earth. It has an average salinity of 40%, compared to a global average of 35%. The close proximity of various low islands, sandbars and reefs translate to a relatively small tidal range for its beaches.

The Red Sea is home to a richly diverse eco-system, which includes around 1200 species of fish. There are 42 different deep water species and 44 different species of shark. Its coast is lined by 2,000km of coral reef, which represents about 200 species of soft and hard coral. Visibility is good and the region has very little sign of coral bleaching. It is hardly surprising that the area is very popular with diving enthusiasts.

Diving Preparation

If you are planning to do some diving in the Red Sea in or around Hurghada, there are a few things you should bear in mind. Diving Companies in the area are meticulous about safety precautions. Before being allowed to dive, you will need to submit a PADI Medical Statement form. You should also have a valid medical certificate, no older than twelve months stating that you are fit to dive.

Experienced divers are strongly advised to have their diving cards, logbooks and any valid documentation handy to prove their proficiency levels. Beginner divers should bear in mind that they will be required to complete an introductory course before being allowed on an excursion in the sea. If they have booked a dive, but failed to achieve the required proficiency level, they will not be allowed out on a dive, even if they have booked and paid in advance. Various packages and diving courses are available and Egyptian diving instructors and guides are generally highly rated.

Reef Diving

Although Careless Reef is only accessible by boat, it offers a colorful dive that will include an abundance of marine wildlife, such as morays, blue-spotted rays and turtles. The two coral towers located at 16m are favorite hangouts for the resident moray eel population.

Gota Abu Ramada, also known as The Aquarium, is accessible via boat ride and features a diverse abundance of marine species. These include angelfish, parrotfish, butterfly fish, triggerfish, eagle rays, anthias, snappers and sweetlips. The western side of the reef is marked by two coral towers. The area is great for underwater photography, but can get quite crowded with other divers during the peak holiday season in August and September.

Shabrour Siyul goes by the alternate name of Blind Reef, as the reef is partially hidden. The area features various shallow caves and is populated by triggerfish, angelfish, glassfish and turtles. The coral growth includes fire coral and black coral. The current can be tricky, though, particularly upon ascent.

Sha'ab Abu Nugar or "father of the pools", consists of a fairly large T-shaped reef with inner lagoons or "pools". It has a particularly large variety of corals, including yellow and purple gorgonians, seafans and brain coral. Besides the usual reef dwellers such as parrotfish and angelfish, it also hosts turtles and bottlenose dolphins.

Shipwreck Diving

Besides coral reefs, Hurghada also offers divers the chance to explore a variety of nearby shipwrecks. One of the more spectacular of these, is the *El Mina*, also known as the Harbour Wreck. This 70m minesweeper from Egypt was a casualty of the Six Day War, and went down in 1969, after a fatal altercation with an Israeli fighter plane.

Its aircraft guns and ammunition are still clearly visible, but the ship has since been colonized by glassfish, moray, shrimp, barracuda, clownfish, sea urchins and anemones. Do bear in mind that the currents can be deceptive and the ship's position is considered unstable. Although fairly near to Hurghada's harbour, this wreck can be difficult to locate.

Smaller and more recent, the *Excalibur* is a 21m safari boat that went down in 1995. It already shows early development of soft coral and also hosts the occasional dolphin or turtle. Other marine residents include lionfish, glassfish and sea horses. It can be found a few hundred meters from Ramoza beach, but its placement is still considered unstable. At 33m lies Mohammed Hasabella, a fishing trawler.

A particularly rich opportunity can be grasped at the site known as Sha'ab Abu Nuhas. Its triangle shape reef provided a final resting place for no less than four major ship wrecks. The most interesting of these, is without a doubt the *Carnatic*, a grand old lady of British origin, who went down in September 1869. The *Carnatic* was a passenger and mail ship and according to records, she carried a rich cargo of gold bullion, as well as a shipment of wine. Today her decaying cabins and decks are furnished with coral and inhabited by a families of grouper, glassfish, moray and jacks. This is one of the most popular diving locations around Hurghada. Other wrecks of Sha-ab Abu Nuhas include the *Chrisoula K*, a large Greek cargo ship that sank in 1981, an even larger Greek freighter, the *Giannis D*, which, at over 100m is one of the larger wrecks in the area, and *Kimon M*, a large German vessel that went down in December 1978.

Some of the deeper lying wrecks are recommended for more experienced divers. The reef at Sha'ab Ruhr Umm Gamar houses several wrecks, including the *Colona IV* at approximately 70m. One recently discovered wreck is that of the ferry, *Al Qamar Al Saudi Al Misri*, which goes as deep as 83m.

Giftun Islands

http://www.getyourguide.com/hurghada-l403/full-day-snorkeling-trip-to-giftun-island-from-hurghada-t10954/

Also known as Mahmya or Paradise Islands, the Giftun Islands had been declared a protected marine park. It is a popular attraction for day trips from Hurghada. The area can only be reached by boat, but offers an underwater eden of crystal clear water and an abundance of colorful coral growth and fish species. As the current is fairly weak and the waters quite shallow, it provides a safe environment for less experienced divers. The water depth reaches 25m. Snorkelling is equally popular. Do pack plenty of sunblock, sunglasses and bottled water, as the island offers very little shade. The island can be very hot, particularly from June to September. Most tour operators provide a buffet lunch as part of the package and have snorkelling gear available. Expect to pay around $55.

Diving Locations Nearby

If you are looking for a diving location that is relatively unspoilt and a little less crowded, consider a trip to Marsa Alam, which is about two and a half hour's drive from Hurghada.

There are sites suitable for beginners and more experienced divers, including coral reefs and shallow wrecks. The coastal reef of Abu Dabab offers sanctuary to some of the region's green turtles, whereas Shaab Samadai lets you explore an interesting collection of caves. Here too, you can expect to encounter spinner dolphins. At Elphinstone Reef sharks are on patrol. Emperor Divers (http://www.emperordivers.com) offers a day's diving in the area for $82.

Shadwan Island, in the Strait of Gubal, has been the site of bitter struggle between Egypt and Israel on various occasions, but it also features a fascinating coral reef that goes 40m deep and is inhabited by snappers, reef sharks, hawksbill turtles and dolphins.

Resorts near Hurghada

Makadi Bay

Located about 30km south of Hurghada, Makadi Bay consists mainly of hotels and other tourist facilities, without any local settlements nearby. The bay is set between sand dunes, against the backdrop of the Red Sea Mountains and has been developed as a tranquil self-contained village suitable for family groups and individuals looking for peace and quiet.

There are restaurants and bars that offer live music, but this is somewhat more subdued, if compared to Hurghada's city center. The beaches are mostly sandy, but the proximity of coral reefs mean that there is a possibility of sharp rocks. The area offers great diving potential and other activities include wind-surfing, beach volleyball, golf, tennis, horse-riding and camel-riding.

One of its major underwater attractions is the Fort Arabesque reef. Easily accessible from the beach through a short stroll, this is a great site for basic snorkelling. I Dive (http://www.idivedivingcenter.com/), an IDC PEDI accredited diving center operates in the Makadi Bay region and will be able to organize excursions to a number of sites, including the island of Abu Hashish, formerly a smugglers' den, but now thankfully only inhabited by the likes of turtles, squids, mackerel, rays and moray eel, the Royal Garden and the incredibly diverse Gota Abu Ramada.

El Gouna

Located about 22km from Hurghada International Airport, El Gouna consists of a collection of about 20 islands, interlinked with picturesque bridges and surrounded by scenic lagoons. The two main beaches are Zeytuna and Mangroovy Beach and the area has facilities for a large selection of water sports including windsurfing, kitesurfing, parasailing, snorkelling and water skiing.

There are seventeen hotels, a wide selection of shops, bars and restaurants, as well as a golf course and three marinas. Other attractions include a go-kart track, a paintball arena, a football stadium that can seat 12,000, tennis courts, horse-riding stables, an aquarium and a small museum.

The museum houses about 90 exhibits, which includes replicas of ancient sculptures and statues and artefacts such as musical instruments. There is also a selection of contemporary paintings by Hussein Bikar, who is regarded as one of Egypt's most important artists of the 20th century. It is housed in the Kafr El Gouna building. Various souvenir shops near the museum sell replicas of ancient Egyptian sculptures, papyrus art, post cards and books on Egypt.

Sahl Hasheesh

Located 18km from Hurghada, Sahl Hasheesh is a modern, well-maintained resort settlement, but one of its biggest attractions is the sunken city. This underwater feature can be seen from the walkway leading towards the docks, but the best way to experience its labyrinth of columns and other features, is by diving. The seafront is lined by a paved boardwalk. Another distinctive feature of the Sahl Hasheesh resort is the "Pharaonic Gate", made as a replica of the temple gate of Karnac. It is lined by an honor guard of ancient soldier statues.

Soma Bay

Located 45km south of Hurghada's international airport on a beautiful peninsula, Soma Bay is an exclusive resort consisting of about five main hotels. The development includes a well-designed marina, a golf course designed by Gary Player and a highly rated health spa, Les Thermes Marins des Cascades, that offers thalasso therapy. Soma Bay features a wide lagoon, enclosed almost completely by surrounding coral reef. This calm and sheltered environment, known for its clear waters, provides an ideal setting for beginner divers to learn the craft and gain some confidence.

Port Safaga

Safaga is located about 53km south of Hurghada. Originally named Philotera, the port was founded in the 3rd century BC. It is mainly a merchant port, but does have some tourist facilities, as it is popular with windsurfers and kite-surfers. The waters here carry high concentrations of salt and other minerals and are considered to be beneficial for the skin. Its bay is flanked by a chain of reefs known collectively as Tobia Arbaa. These include the Panorama Reef, as well as the Abu Quifan Reef, both home to populations of tuna, sharks and mantas.

The area offers a unique challenge to more advanced divers. This is the wreck of the *Salem Express*, a ferry that travelled between Jeddah, Saudi Arabia and Egypt carrying pilgrims returning from Mecca. It went down in December 1991 near Hyndeman reef, with a death toll of around 470 people. The wreck now lies at a depth of between 39m and 108m and is recommended only for experienced divers. Many of the fittings are still very recognizable and amongst the debris lie some of the possessions of its unfortunate passengers.

Nightlife in Hurghada

The most popular night time hangout for divers is Papas Bar, which is located on the marina. Papas Beach Club (El Sakia Beach, Sekala) offers you the unique experience of dancing on the beach under the stars. One of Hurghada's first bars is the Dutch-run Peanuts Bar, which is located in the El Dahar neighborhood. It is a favorite with locals and tourists and offers free Wi-Fi coverage, karaoke nights and a friendly atmosphere.

Those in search of a somewhat livelier entertainment scene, could stop off at the Ministry of Sound, Hed Kandi on the Marina or the Hard Rock Cafe. Hed Kandi hosts vibrant beach entertainment with powerful sound, innovative decor and professional DJs and dance crews. In the season, events are attended by thousands of revellers.

The cocktails are also of a high standard. Based on the original club in London, Ministry of Sound now has branded outlets in various locations around the world, including Egypt. During the peak holiday season, the Hurghada outlet is packed with clubbers enjoying vibe and music played by world class DJs, which is primarily house or R&B. If you are more into rock music, head over to the Hard Rock Cafe, which offers great live entertainment, good food and wonderful cocktails. The Hard Rock Cafe is located along on the coastal Alkora Road in the Alnawara Center and, as with most of the brand, the venue includes an interesting assortment of rock memorabilia. Calypso Disco is a large dance venue, that offers free drinks along with the admission. The music is mainly house, techno and trance.

Day Trips

Some of Egypt's world-famous historical sights can be accessed as a day trip or a few days' excursion from Hurghada. The most famous of these is of course Luxor, described as the greatest open-air museum on the planet. The site includes various ancient sites such as the city of Thebes with the iconic image of the temple of Hatshepsut, the Valley of Kings, the Valley of Queens and the ruins at Karnac. A trip to Cairo could include a visit to the Great Pyramid at Giza and the enigmatic Sphinx. Tours can be booked singly or in combination from Hurghada.

Equally fascinating, but a little nearer is El Quesir, a port city dating back at least 3500 years. Its harbour is ancient, and the city also has a fortress dating back to the Ottoman era. El Quesir is about 80km south of Hurghada, on the way to Marsa Alam.

Recommendations for the Budget Traveller

Places to Stay

Triton Empire Inn

Hospital & Sayed Korrayem St., Hurghada, Egypt

Located conveniently near the beach, Triton Empire Inn has a large swimming pool, restaurant and bar/lounge.

There is live poolside entertainment in the evening and the wellness center has a sauna, jacuzzi and offers massage treatments. Individual rooms come equipped with a fridge, satellite TV, safe, balcony and air-conditioning. Rooms are kept clean and well-maintained. Staff members are friendly and speak several languages. Accommodation begins at $35 and includes a buffet breakfast.

Movenpick Resort Hurghada

El Fareek Youssef Affifi Street,
Hurghada, Egypt
(Formerly Continental Resort Hurghada)
http://www.moevenpick-hotels.com/en/africa/egypt/hurghada/resort-hurghada/location/

Movenpick Resort is located in the Hurghada Bay, approximately 7km from the city center. The hotel has its own private beach, which is connected to an artificial island via a bridge, as well as a garden and a swimming pool. There is a restaurant, bar/lounge, business center, fitness and wellness center. Tennis courts are available and activities such as horse-riding and water sports can be arranged. There is also a special programme for children. Facilities are wheelchair friendly and live entertainment is provided. All rooms include a mini-bar, air-conditioning, hairdryer, satellite TV and internet access. Wi-Fi is available in the public areas. Accommodation begins at $54 and includes breakfast.

Sol y Mar Ivory Suites

El Kawsar District, Hurghada, Egypt
Tel: +20-(0) 65 3462 610

Sol y Mar Ivory Suites is located about 1km from the airport of Hurghada and within walking distance of the city center. There is a swimming pool and lobby bar. At a small extra fee, the hotel offers an additional convenience - access to the facilities of its sister hotel, Iberotel Aquamarine, which is a five star establishment. This includes a shuttle service and the use of a health spa, as well as eight different restaurants. All units are spacious and well-maintained and include a kitchenette, bathroom facilities, satellite TV, internet access, a safe, minibar and a balcony or terrace. Accommodation begins at $45 a night.

Magawish Swiss Inn Resort

Safaga Road, Hurghada, Egypt
Tel: +20 65 346 46 20/1/2
http://www.swissinn.net/magawish/index.htm

Magawish Swiss Inn Resort is the oldest hotel in Hurghada and dates back to 1976. It has access to one of the best beaches in Hurghada and is located within close proximity of a well known wind-surfing and kite surfing center. There are two swimming pools and other activities available include horseriding, tennis, squash and diving.

A sauna room and massage services are also available. The hotel offers several restaurant options including the Mermaid restaurant, which specializes in seafood and the main eatery, the Manta restaurant where buffet style dining can be enjoyed, as well as several pool bars, an Oriental cafe and a disco. Rooms include air-conditioning, satellite TV, a bathtub or shower, and a terrace or balcony. Various types of accommodation is available, ranging from basic rooms to studios, apartments, bungalows and villas. Accommodation begins at $53 a night.

Festival Riviera

km 11 Ahiaa Rd - North Hurghada, Hurghada 249, Egypt

Although Festival Riviera is not located near the shopping areas, it does offer access to the beach and plenty of fun beachside attractions such as henna tattoos, a beach bar and Oscar, the hotel's resident camel.

There is a swimming pool, bar/lounge, restaurant and a well-maintained garden area to relax in. Rooms are clean, spacious and comfortable and include television and an en suite bathroom. Internet access is charged as an optional extra. There are special activities for children and facilities for gym, volleyball and more. Accommodation begins at $56.

Places to Eat

Nubian Cafe & Restaurant

Marina Hurghada, Hurghada, Egypt
Tel: 0122287825

Located along the trendy Hurghada Marina development, the Nubian Cafe & Restaurant offers its patrons great dining while enjoying a view of some of the area's luxury yachts. The food is an authentically Egyptian blend of North African and Asian cuisine. Some of the dishes include lamb kebabs, falafel, the versatile aubergine based favorite baba ganoush, mudammas and molokhiyya. The camel liver served here is said to be exceptional and other items include lamb chops, mixed grill, camel steak, fried squid and seafood platter. Service is friendly. Additional pleasures include the hibiscus tea and the hookah pipe. Expect to pay around $20 per person for a meal plus drinks.

El Mina Restaurant

El Minaa St., Hurghada 22313, Egypt
Tel: +20 65 3556637

El Mina is one of the oldest fish restaurants in Hurghada and its main speciality is seafood. Diners may be offered the opportunity to select their own fish and choose whether they want it fried or grilled. The seafood soup is described as excellent value for money. Meals are served with salad, rice, chips and grilled vegetables. There is a coffee shop on the third floor where diners can also enjoy shisha. Prices are reasonable.

The Lodge Restaurant

Hurghada Marina, Hurghada 1200EG, Egypt
Tel: +20168831438

Located on the Hurghada marina, the Lodge restaurant offers live music, great atmosphere and friendly service. It is mainly a grill restaurant and some of the menu items include surf and turf, chicken skewers with peanut sauce, chicken pasta and camel steak. There is also a kids' menu. Expect to pay around $18.50 for a starter, main dish plus drinks per person.

Moby Dick

Sheraton Road, Hurghada, Egypt
Tel: 653440050
http://www.mobydick-egypt.com/about.htm

Moby Dick started out modestly in 2003 as a restaurant with beer garden on the popular shopping street, Sheraton Road and expanded to earn catering contracts with several airlines servicing Egypt. They are well-known for their excellent camel steak, served with lyonaisse potatoes and a choice of pepper or mushroom sauce. There are other choices on the menu such as sea bass, calamari and sweet and sour chicken. Service is friendly. Expect to pay around $20 per person for a main meal plus drinks.

La Trattoria

Paradise Village
Village Road 11, Hurghada, Egypt
Tel: 01284046098

If after a while, the halal cuisine of Egypt has you slightly nostalgic for a few rashers of bacon or some ham, consider going Italian. Besides guilty Western pleasures, La Trattoria offers relaxing poolside dining on the terrace, as well as indoor seating.

The mixed antipasti platter consists of cheeses and cold cuts, served with focaccia bread. Main meal staples are pizza and pasta, as well as meat, fish and chicken from the grill. Open for lunch and supper, the restaurant offers a relaxing environment and great value for money.

Places to Shop

Downtown Bazaar

The Downtown Bazaar is one of Hurghada's biggest markets and here you will find a large variety of goods spread out at the resident stalls. The goods range from electronic equipment and factory made toys, to textiles, scarves, clothing, jewellery, handbags, shoes, carpets and rugs. Among the crafted items you can also expect pottery and carvings. There are several stalls selling shisha pipes, a popular indulgence in Hurghada. Other items include perfume, spices, fast food and juice.

Hurghada Star Shop

Located on the Promenade near Siva Grand Beach Hotel and Hotel Sindbad, Hurghada Star Shop is a large shop that sells a wide selection of souvenirs and gifts. It is spread across two floors and provides a relaxing environment where potential shoppers can browse at leisure, without being pressured into a sale, by the aggressive sales pitch of over-eager vendors.

Some of the items include clothing, T-shirts, shoes, slippers, jewellery, diving gear, books, postcards, toys, handbags and towels. You can also choose from a wide variety of typically Egyptian items such as shisha pipes, papyrus or carvings featuring some of Egypt's most distinctive deities and artefacts. Prices are reasonable, but fixed. If you want to haggle, go elsewhere.

Shopping at the New Marina

Al Nol (Tel: 0122151062) means "the loom" and this shop, located on the trendy New Marina development, specializes in fiber arts, offering a wide variety of Egyptian crafted cloth and textile products. If you are looking for the famous Egyptian cotton, you have come to the right place. Here, you will be able to choose from bed spreads, shawls, scarves and hand woven table cloths. There is also a range of imported camel hair products from Iraq, as well as traditional dresses. Other items include Bedouin glassware, copper and brass items, candle holders, handbags, make-up bags and tiffany lamps.

The New Marina has its own souk section, where visitors can experience the sights and scents of a typical market place. Some of the goods you can look for in the souq include handbags and other leather accessories, clothing, including scarves, beaded and embroidered garments and galabias, or traditional dresses for various occasions, pottery and mirrors from Morocco and also brassware, such as candle holders, plates and vases and jewellery and ornaments crafted from silver, amber, amethyst, malachite, onyx, tiger's eye, lapis lazuli, jasper and topaz.

Egyptian perfume goes back 4000 years, and within the souq you can browse till heart's content among the oils and perfumes, sampling fragrances with names such as Nefertiti, Hatshepsut, Secret of the Desert, Papyrus and Lotus. Speaking of papyrus, it is one of the most popular souvenirs amongst tourists.

A favorite keepsake is the basic sheet which contains the hieroglyphic alphabet. Additionally, there are stalls selling shisha pipes, spices and replicas of ancient Egyptian art and statues. There is also an African gallery, which sells art and artefacts from various locations in Africa.

Senzo Mall

A new mall that offers Egyptians and tourists a variety of shopping choices is Senzo Mall, which opened in 2009 and is now the city's largest shopping mall. There are several outlets for branded shops such as Adidas, Tommy Hilfiger and Calvin Klein, as well as other shops selling T-shirts, other clothing and souvenir items. There is a food hall, as well as fun activities such as go-karting and a play area for children. The mall also has free wireless internet. Do bear in mind that the prices are fixed.

Foodies may wish to pay a visit to Spinneys, in Senzo Mall, which stocks a range of imported and local speciality items. These include organic, sugar free and gluten free products. You can expect to find pastas, chocolates, biscuits, cereal, Buffalo Mozzarella and salami from Italy, Emmenthaler cheese from Switzerland, Italian ice cream and real Swiss chocolate.

Cleopatra Center

opposite Waves Beach Resort, Sekella

In Egypt, sellers are aggressive hagglers. If you are looking for a slightly more relaxing shopping environment and are willing to accept a fixed price structure, you will probably have a great time at the Cleopatra Center. It is located in the Sekella neighborhood and here you may find Egyptian gifts and souvenirs such as plates and ashtrays, leather, jewellery, handbags, postcards and T-shirts and towels of Egyptian cotton. There is a whole perfume department and also toys, books and snorkelling equipment. The center is spread across four storeys.

Printed in Great Britain
by Amazon